DR. GLORIA I. SAN MIGUEL

BOOK SERIES BY FIG FACTOR MEDIA

WordPower Book Series

© Copyright 2023, Fig Factor Media, LLC.
All rights reserved.

All rights reserved. No portion of this book may be reproduced by mechanical, photographic or electronic process, nor may it be stored in a retrieval system, transmitted in any form or otherwise be copied for public use or private use without written permission of the copyright owner.

It is sold with the understanding that the publisher and the individual authors are not engaged in the rendering of psychological, legal, accounting or other professional advice. The content and views in each chapter are the sole expression and opinion of its author and not necessarily the views of Fig Factor Media, LLC.

For more information, contact:

Fig Factor Media, LLC | www.figfactormedia.com

Cover Design & Layout by Juan Pablo Ruiz
Printed in the United States of America

ISBN: 978-1-959989-51-6

DEDICATION

I dedicate this book, first and foremost, to our Lord and Savior, Jesus Christ, who has been so faithful in my life. To my Heavenly Father, who planted the first seed of an idea and watered it as it continued to grow.

"Above all else, guard your heart, for everything you do flows from it." (Proverbs 4:23, NIV)

"From my birth, I have relied on you; you brought me forth from my mother's womb. I will ever praise you." (Psalm 71:6, NIV)

Thank you, God, for dictating this book to my heart!

ACKNOWLEDGMENTS

I am deeply grateful to my husband Javier and daughters, Giselle and Desiree, for their love and support. My maternal grandmother, Monserrate Santiago, raised me with love, and I cherish her influence on my life. To my aunt, Emilia Lamboy, thank you for always being there for me. My parents, Mildred Lamboy and Jose Perez taught me the power of forgiveness and transformation through faith in Christ.

A special shoutout to my dear friend, Mariselis Crespo, whose friendship has been a blessing. To my friends (I wish I can mention all of you by name, but the word count is limiting here—you all know who you are) for their heartfelt support and for traveling around the path of life with me. Anitza San Miguel thank you for introducing me to Jackie Camacho. Jackie, your divine downloads are very aligned with mine and your team has been amazing in supporting my dream to publish.

I extend my thanks to my friend, Pastor Dr. Ruth Marie Calderon from Re.Live Church. To my extended family, pastors, and churches, your prayers and spiritual support mean the world to me. Thank you to Pastor Dr. Denise Salasblanca, Pastors Ernesto Balvaneda and Cristina Garcia, Pastors Bernardo and Monica Javier, Rvdo. Hector Santiago and Isabel Rolon for your prayers and spiritual support.

Appreciation to mentors and teachers—John Maxwell, Paul Martinelli, Elsa Ilardo, John Mejia, Misael Diaz, Mrs. Raquel Bruno, Dr. Marie H. Delmestre, Dr. Jose R. Ortiz, Mrs. Maria C. Gutierrez—for guidance and inspiration. My Maxwell Leadership, Empowered Living, and Kairos Global families redirected me to purpose.

Lastly, heartfelt thanks to my beloved readers. Sharing my story brings immense satisfaction, your reception is a grounding gift. Thank you from my heart!

INTRO

Heart is a book born from the author's profound desire to help others through counseling. With a background in cardiology and oncology, the heart has always held a central place in her personal and professional life. After fervently praying for a meaningful topic, she was inspired to write about the heart not just as a physical organ, but as the source of love, compassion, and kindness.

The book's essence lies in sharing heartfelt advice, transcending mere stories to offer wisdom and inspiration. It acts as a loving guide, addressing emotional, physical, and spiritual healing. The pages intertwine themes to convey a powerful and inspiring message, aiming to enrich the lives of readers.

Heart also raises awareness about cardiovascular and heart diseases, which often remain silent killers. Through personal and fictional anecdotes, the book emphasizes the importance of heart health, while safeguarding the privacy of the individuals involved. It tenderly recounts the sudden loss of the author's mother to a heart attack, paying tribute to her memory, and shares the author's own journey through a recent heart attack.

Overflowing with the authentic love of God, *Heart* reaches out to touch lives, offering solace and guidance in a world where emotions and well-being often intertwine. Its powerful message not only serves as inspiration but also provides vital knowledge to safeguard heart health and nurture the goodness within each individual's heart.

MY STORY

From an early age, I cherished learning and knowledge, a tribute to the love and care imparted to me by my grandmother and aunt. Their influence instilled in me the belief that knowledge was invaluable and could never be taken away. I understood that my circumstances wouldn't define me, and I could shape my future by striving to be a better person.

Throughout my journey, I received valuable support and advice from various sources, including family, teachers, mentors, and even strangers who became role models. While self-belief is essential, sometimes, it takes heartfelt advice to truly recognize our worth and potential. In my case, that advice was always present but came to light in my twenties.

I grew up in the humble neighborhood of Tokio in Hato Rey, Puerto Rico, where my family was displaced, to the Sabana Hoyos neighborhood in Vega Alta. I remember that God always put opportunities in my path to discover that there was something better and greater for me. Not because I was ungrateful, but because He had advice for my heart from his heart.

I encountered divine opportunities that revealed greater possibilities for me. God's guidance and wisdom became paramount in my life, safeguarding my heart and directing my steps. Though I faced uncertainty at times, I persevered with renewed strength through prayer, always pressing toward the goal set by God and Christ.

By entrusting my life, desires, and thoughts to God, I remained on the path to eternal life with unwavering faith. Each step I took was guided by my Heavenly Father, giving me the courage to overcome challenges and continue toward my purpose in life. With gratitude and determination, I embrace this journey with God as my eternal companion.

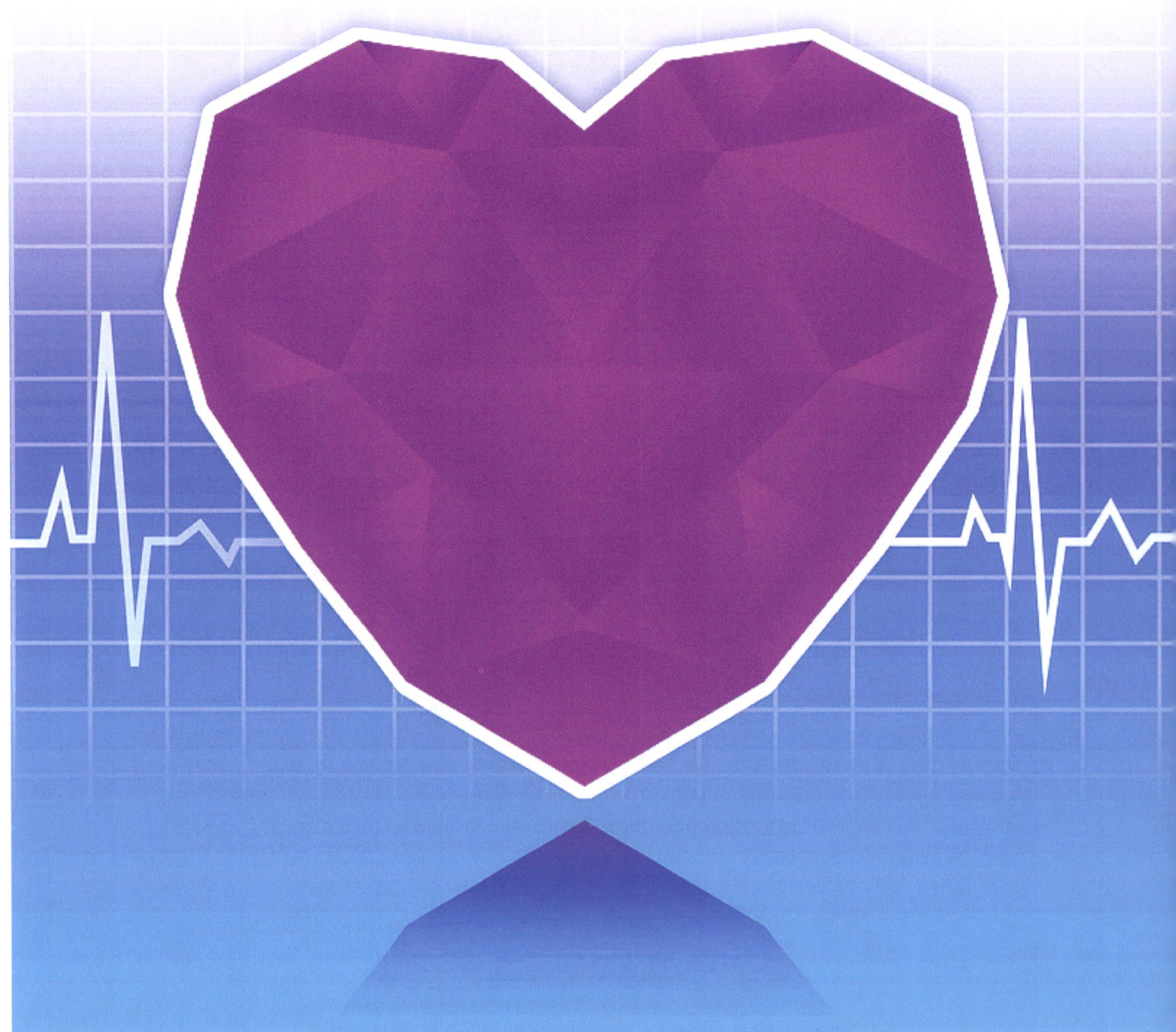

ABOUT HEART DISEASE IN WOMEN

This cause is dear and close to my heart. My mother passed away unexpectedly from a heart attack. Heart disease and stroke kill 1 out of 3 women, but the American Heart Association[1] said these deaths are often preventable through awareness, lifestyle changes, and medical supervision. So many people have this silent disease. We must raise awareness of heart disease in women. The signs and symptoms are different for women than for men, and may not be easily noticed.

Heart attack symptoms for women:
The most common heart attack symptom in women is the same as in men—some type of chest pain, pressure, or discomfort that lasts more than a few minutes, or comes and goes. But chest pain is not always severe or even the most noticeable symptom, particularly in women. Women often describe heart attack pain as pressure or tightness.

Below are some symptoms women might experience in addition to chest pain[2]:
- Neck, jaw, shoulder, upper back, or upper belly discomfort
- Shortness of breath
- Pain in one or both arms
- Nausea or vomiting
- Sweating
- Lightheadedness or dizziness
- Unusual fatigue
- Heartburn

These symptoms may not be as noticeable as the crushing chest pain often associated with heart attacks. That is why when I had unusual shoulder pain, something told me to go get it checked. Compared with men, women tend to have symptoms more often when resting, or even when asleep. Emotional stress can play a role in triggering heart attack symptoms in women. Because women's heart attack symptoms can differ from men's, women may be diagnosed less often.

---

[1] "The Facts about Women and Heart Disease," Go Red for Women, 2023, https://www.goredforwomen.org/en/about-heart-disease-in-women.
[2] "The Facts about Women and Heart Disease," Go Red for Women, 2023, https://www.goredforwomen.org/en/about-heart-disease-in-women.

MY HEART JOURNEY

In 2019, I lost my mother suddenly to a heart attack, prompting me to raise awareness about heart disease in women. Concerned about the hereditary aspect, I consulted a cardiologist and adopted a healthier lifestyle. After two years of monitoring, I was discharged with a clean bill of health, proud of my weight loss and fitness progress.

However, three months later, after a strenuous workout, I experienced unusual shoulder pain. Remembering the warning signs for women, I sought medical attention immediately. I thought about my mom and everything I had learned as part of being an advocate for Go Red for Women campaign for the American Heart Association. Women have different symptoms than men and it's possible to have a heart attack without chest pain.

I went to Urgent Care because I wasn't feeling well. The initial tests seemed fine, but my troponin levels were high, which can indicate a heart problem. Because of this, they quickly took me to the hospital. They performed several tests, but couldn't figure out exactly what was wrong. Eventually, they did a special type of scan called a heart MRI, which showed that I have a condition called non-ischemic hypertrophic cardiomyopathy. It's a thickening of the heart muscle that's not caused by a lack of blood flow. Interestingly, when they put a catheter into my heart to check for blockages, they didn't find any.

My journey with this condition continues, but I remain steadfast in my faith, trusting that my life is in the hands of the Lord. I hope to share my experience to educate others about heart health and inspire them to listen to their bodies and take proactive steps for their well-being.

MAMI'S EULOGY

In Memory of Mildred Lamboy 1/31/58-9/14/19

First of all, I want to thank God for his infinite goodness and mercy. For his peace that surpasses all understanding because his will and timing are perfect. Thanks to all of you, family and friends, gathered here and those who accompany us in thought, prayer, and heart. All of you who have supported us in one way or another, many names to mention, you know who you are.

Mami passed away unexpectedly before our eyes, but I am sure that God has a purpose for her departure. He acts in mysterious ways, but He shows His will and favor at all times. What can I tell you… God allowed Mami to spare her death on two occasions due to car accidents. This time He called her, in her bedroom in the middle of the night.

Her life was very difficult, but in the last 17 years, she gave testimony with her life to the value of forgiveness, gratitude, redemption, and reconciliation. She is my best friend, my confidant, and the best grandmother for our girls, always cheerful and playful… full of jokes and joy; we are going to miss her the world.

Mami, the sky is not the limit, but the beginning!

Thanks to everyone who has shared stories with Mami, her jokes and occurrences, and especially how she ministered to your life in difficult times through the Word of God and Prayer.

Her beautiful, helpful heart remains with us forever, you will always live in our hearts. We love you!

COPING WITH GRIEF: HEALING YOUR HEART FROM A LOSS

Grief is a deeply personal and intricate emotion, following the loss of a loved one, relationship, or cherished dream. It encompasses sorrow, sadness, anger, guilt, and confusion, with each person's experience shaped by their unique background and coping mechanisms. Acceptance is the first step in healing, acknowledging, and validating feelings rather than suppressing them. Building a support network through friends, family, or grief support groups can provide comfort.

Expressing emotions healthily through activities like writing, art, or exercise can be therapeutic. Healing is not linear, and setbacks and sadness may still occur after acceptance. Self-compassion is crucial, being patient and kind during recovery without self-judgment. Professional help through counseling or therapy can aid in processing emotions and memories.

Honoring the memory of the loved one is essential, celebrating their life and preserving the moments shared. Rituals and ceremonies offer closure and connection. As time passes, grief may transform into bittersweet remembrance rather than overwhelming sorrow. It is okay to find joy and meaning in life while holding space for the memories of the past.

Grief cannot be "solved" but becomes a part of who we are, fostering resilience and compassion. The pain may never fully disappear, but it becomes more manageable with support and time. Everyone's grief journey is unique, and there is no right or wrong way to grieve. Respecting one's own process is crucial. By embracing emotions, seeking support, and practicing self-compassion, individuals can navigate grief and find hope and healing in their hearts.

FIVE KEYS TO FORGIVING FROM THE HEART

Forgiveness doesn't mean the absence of pain, but a willingness to let go of resentment and anger. It's accepting that others, like us, can be wrong and deserving of compassion. It's a commitment to change and healing. Here are five keys to practice forgiveness:

1. Choose love over grudges. Holding onto grudges will destroy your soul like acid, while forgiveness heals like removing a tumor.
2. Choose compassion over revenge. Put yourself in others' shoes, understanding their regret or weakness. Revenge only poisons the heart.
3. Choose growth over stagnation. Forgiveness should lead to maturity and strength. It allows you to love more deeply and consciously.
4. Choose humility over arrogance. Recognize your imperfections and the potential for making similar mistakes.
5. Choose God's strength over your own. Forgiving from the heart is possible through the love and compassion of Jesus.

By practicing these choices, forgiveness becomes a transformative process that liberates you from the burden of anger and resentment, leading to personal growth and inner peace.

HEALING A BROKEN HEART

Healing a broken heart is a challenging process that requires proper care and understanding. The emotions experienced during heartbreak, like sadness, disappointment, and pain, can be overwhelming, but there are effective ways to cope and move forward.

Neuroscientist Lucy Brown explains that the brain processes heartbreak similarly to hunger or thirst, making it difficult to suppress intense feelings.[3] However, there are steps one can take to facilitate healing:[4]

1. Rebuilding Self-Concept: Counter self-blame and emptiness by restoring self-identity and worth.
2. "Zero Contact" Rule: Break contact to ease grieving and create emotional space.
3. Self-Care: Prioritize physical and mental well-being through exercise, nutrition, and rest.
4. Patience and Acceptance: Allow time to process emotions and come to terms with the situation.
5. Seek Support: Friends offer comfort and distraction, fostering normalcy and joy.

In conclusion, healing a broken heart requires nurturing oneself, seeking support, and practicing patience and acceptance. It's a gradual process, but with self-compassion and determination, one can grow and move beyond the pain, finding happiness and fulfillment once again. Professional help may also be beneficial for those struggling to cope effectively. Remember, be kind to yourself throughout the journey of healing.

---

[3] "Study Links Romantic Rejection with Reward and Addiction Centers in the Brain," Albert Einstein College of Medicine, July 6, 2010, https://www.einsteinmed.edu/news/releases/546/study-links-romantic-rejection-with-reward-and-addiction-centers-in-the-brain/.

[4] "Study Links Romantic Rejection with Reward and Addiction Centers in the Brain," Albert Einstein College of Medicine, July 6, 2010, https://www.einsteinmed.edu/news/releases/546/study-links-romantic-rejection-with-reward-and-addiction-centers-in-the-brain/.

HEAL YOUR HEART WITH LOVE

- *Be more loving and giving.* Bring happiness and joy into your life and other people's lives. Be generous with your time and money. Try to do one random act of kindness today, even if it is as simple as smiling at someone.

- *Hug and hold hands.* Physical contact has a loving and nurturing ability to instantly improve your mood, reduce levels of stress, and put you at ease. Try to hug at least one person you love every day.

- *Be more playful in your loving relationship.* Remind your partner how much you care for them and make time for them, no matter how busy you are.

- *Love your life and be grateful.* Bring more joy into your life each day. Flirt with life… laugh, dance, sing. Allow yourself to really laugh without holding anything back and simply enjoy this pure laughter.

- *Love yourself and be kind to yourself every day.* Treat yourself like you would another person with whom you are truly in love. The more you love yourself, the better prepared you will be to love others. And the more love you give, the more you will receive.

PEACE IN YOUR HEART

Having peace in your heart means achieving a state of internal harmony and displaying positive attitudes in your daily life. It requires managing life's circumstances and emotional burdens without letting them disrupt your peace. To do this, you must learn to close certain chapters and let go:

1. Leaving everything in its place: Accept that certain things are beyond your control and allow them to unfold naturally.
2. Moving forward with emotional freedom: Have the courage to let go of past hurts and move on without being held back by emotional baggage.
3. Humility to forgive: Acknowledge that everyone is fallible, including yourself, and be willing to forgive others and yourself from the heart.
4. Accepting the impermanence of moments: Understand that nothing lasts forever, so avoid becoming overly attached to routines or customs, and instead approach life with a winning mentality and passion.

To find peace, be prepared for change and difficult times by giving your best effort and living in the moment to the fullest. Letting go of guilt is crucial, as it can disturb your peace of mind.

Learn to let go using these tips:
1. Accept that life moves on, and you can continue your journey.
2. Be brave in saying goodbye and cutting off painful experiences to keep evolving.
3. Recognize that cycles end and new ones begin, so avoid clinging to the past.
4. Trust in God, understanding that he doesn't cause suffering but offers lessons and opportunities for growth.

By embracing these principles, you can find peace within yourself, allowing you to navigate life's challenges with serenity and grace.

OPEN YOUR HEART TO HAPPINESS

Why is happiness so important in your life?

It allows you to feel spectacular! When you are happy inside your body, three types of hormones are generated that will make you feel in a perfect state:
1. Dopamine - In charge of producing pleasure and motivation.
2. Serotonin - In charge of relieving the mood.
3. Endorphin - Causes the feeling of happiness and well-being.

If you are not happy, you will not be able to be passionate. If you are not passionate, you will feel guilty about not pouring your all into the things you do on a regular basis. It is for this reason that happiness is the perfect complement to passion.

When you are happy, you can live fully and grow as a person. Do not confuse happiness with feelings of pleasure, as they are very easy to confuse. This confusion causes many people to become addicted to alcohol, drugs, etc. Any physical dependence is self-deception and can be dangerous for you. In the long term, these self-deceptions are harmful and destructive to your health and inner happiness.

All the things you receive in life are because you believe in God. Scripture reminds us that true happiness comes from our faith, love for God, and our love comes from a caring heart. The only source of happiness is the Lord. "Take delight in the Lord, and he will give you the desires of your heart." (Psalm 37:4, NIV)

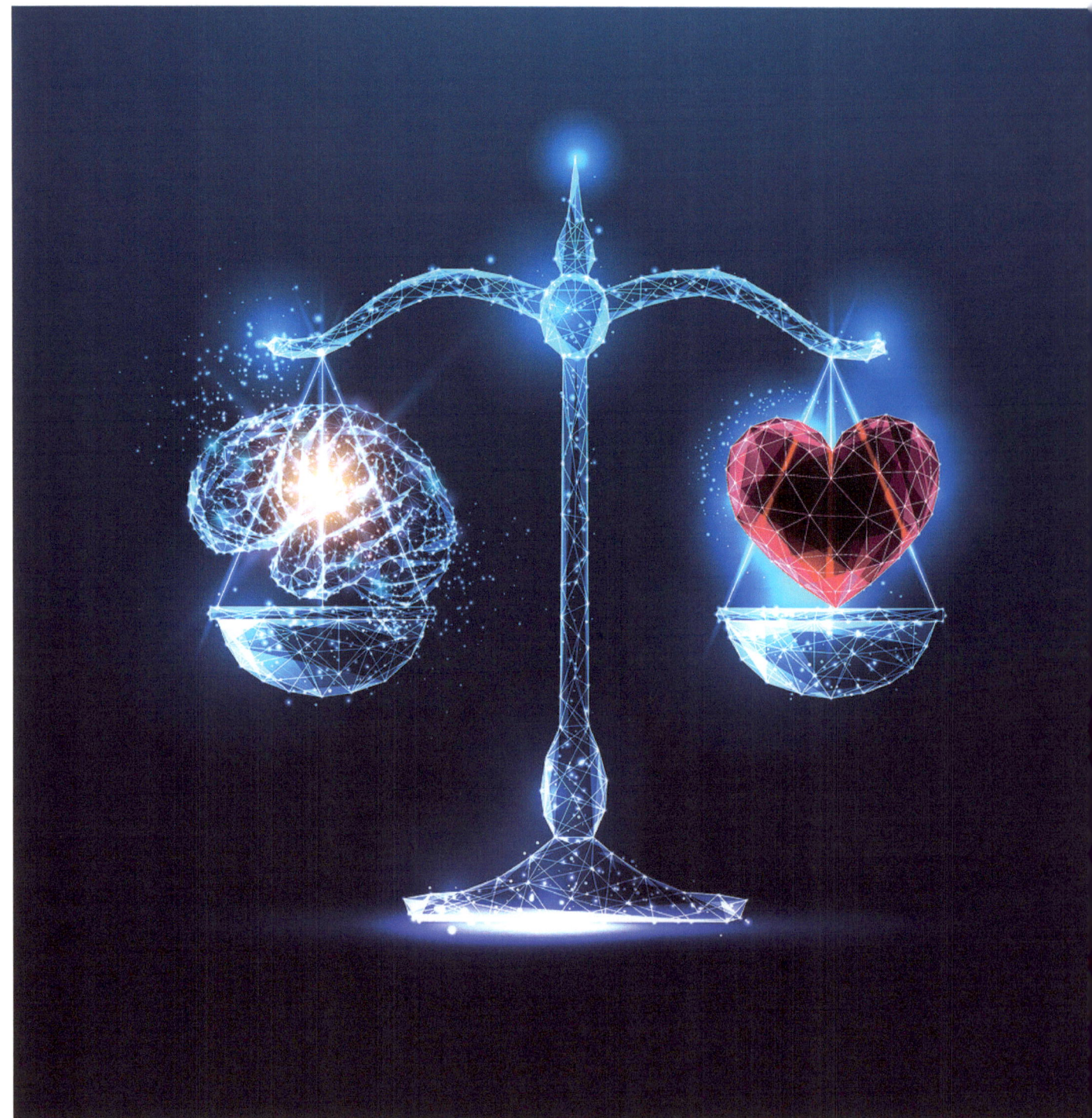

WIN THE BATTLE OF THE MIND WITH A GRATEFUL HEART

Our emotions play a significant role in shaping our mood, behavior, and relationships. However, many are taught to suppress emotions, leading to internal turmoil. The negative thoughts we harbor can become repetitive, reinforcing false beliefs about ourselves and others. Jesus referred to Satan as the 'Father of Lies,' and buying into these deceptions contributes to stress and anxiety. Thankfully, as believers, we have Christ within us to counter these schemes.

To break free from this cycle, we must align our thinking with God's truth. Remembering God's love for us and seeking His wisdom can help us overcome negative thought patterns. Gratitude is a powerful tool to combat negative thinking. By practicing thankfulness regardless of our feelings, appreciating even the small things, finding hidden blessings, and thanking God during challenges, we can shift our focus from problems to His priorities.

Acknowledging and understanding our emotions can improve our relationships and well-being. Rejecting deceptive thoughts and embracing God's truth empowers us to live abundantly. Gratitude serves as a discipline that transforms our minds, leading to a more joyful and fulfilling life.

"I will praise you, Lord, my God, with all my heart." (Psalm 86:12, NIV) This Psalm expresses the heart of thankfulness and glorifying God wholeheartedly.

A LETTER TO MY BELOVED HEART FROM MY WISE HEART

Beloved Heart,

In the complexity of life, always remember to listen to your inner wisdom. Embrace vulnerability, love, and feeling—the essence of existence. Despite joys and challenges, scars mustn't bind you. Love bravely, discerningly. Some bonds aren't forever; release what no longer nourishes. Farewells fuel strength, imperfection holds treasures.

Nurture body and soul; self-love begets boundless love. Heal past wounds without defining yourself by them. You transcend adversities; strength surmounts obstacles.

Be compassionate; mistakes are human. Forgive, learn, and progress. In relationships, honest expression and empathetic listening are paramount.

Time's a gift; love and happiness needn't hurry. Grow at your pace, and guard your heart when needed. The love you give and receive is life's treasure. Embrace risks and new possibilities. Surround yourself with growth and love.

Trust your intuition. You deserve abundant love and happiness. Beat with passion, and live gratefully.

With love and blessings,
Your Wise Heart

ABOUT THE AUTHOR

Dr. Gloria I. San Miguel has over two decades of experience in healthcare clinical operations. Her impressive track record includes serving as a seasoned Healthcare Executive and Vice President of Operations within the medical practice sector. Her expertise encompasses a wide spectrum of healthcare services administration.

Dr. San Miguel was born in Puerto Rico and completed her Bachelor of Science degree in Biology from the University of Puerto Rico. She earned her Master of Science in Healthcare Administration at the University of Central Florida and Doctorate Honoris Causa in Theology from MICAR Christian University.

The author is a certified John Maxwell Leadership transformational coach, healthcare executive, licensed clinical pastoral counselor, entrepreneur, wife, and mother of two teenage girls, living in Central Florida. Her purpose in life is coaching and developing leaders towards living an intentionally driven life and developing the best version of themselves by achieving integral health—emotionally, mentally, spiritually, and physically.

She finds joy in sharing her story of resilience and determination, enriching others' lives with heartfelt guidance as she advances in her career and personal development. She emphasizes the significance of coaches and counselors, taking incremental strides towards achievement, and highlights how her faith has been instrumental in her life's path.

If you need help and/or support, please don't hesitate to reach out to Gloria. She will be happy to add value and help propel you from intention to action in your heart transformation journey!

CONTACT:
Intentionallydrivenbyglory@gmail.com
www.gloriasanmiguel.com
LinkedIn: Gloria San Miguel
Facebook: @crecimientointencional
IG: @intentionallydrivenenterprises

HOW DOES THE WORD **HEART** EMPOWER YOU?

www.ingramcontent.com/pod-product-compliance
Lightning Source LLC
Chambersburg PA
CBHW042055050526
44107CB00110B/1175